To

Holden 4

Let books be your
friends, always!
Cynthia Stephens

Dear Holden,
God Bless!
Enjoy the book.
Jay Robinson
2017

Sacred Ground Productions LLC

Sacred Ground Productions LLC

PO Box 750862 Forest Hills, NY 11375

1. Grief, sadness and loss-Fiction. 2. Grandfather and grandson-Fiction. 3. Death and dying-Fiction. 4. Boy, dog and squirrel-Fiction. 5. Rowboat and oar-Fiction. 6. Lake, swimming, floating-Fiction. 7. Dreaming, sun, moon, stars-Fiction.

ISBN: 1522895140

ISBN 13:978-522895145

Library of Congress Control Number: 2016900402

On Days Like These

Cynthia Stephens

Illustrated by
Cynthia Stephens and Tony Robinson

To my brother, Reni, whose spirit is strong.

I see you.

It was a steamy hot day in the town known as Lockjaw, South Carolina-so called because in the midst of summer it was so hot that no one dared speak too loudly, or breathe too deeply, due to the extreme effort needed. Even the air seemed to sweat, and the spaces below the weeping willows offered no refuge.

So Chester, his dog Cheater, and the squirrel called Pesky lay on their stomachs, their bodies sucking the last bit of coolness from the earth below.

Pesky usually dodged and darted, scampered, and ran circles around them, which amused Chester but annoyed Cheater. But on this day, Pesky kept at a distance, sensing that something was different.

In recent days, Chester could be seen wearing his grandfather's oversized planting hat.
And on this day, Chester's heart was heavy because his grandfather had gone to take his place with the other ancestors.

Chester did not feel up to playing with his friends, but boredom got the best of him, so he went to the place that restored him, on days like these.

Chester went to the lake where he kept the
rowboat his grandfather had given him, the
one with only one oar. He stopped on an
embankment near the shore and laid his body
at the gnarly feet of a huge old oak tree,
pretending that they were his grandfather's feet.

This was the place where Chester had sat with
his grandfather, who would feed him bits of
food from his carving tool while telling him stories
about the old trees that had witnessed many
lives over many lifetimes. But today, there would
be no stories and no bits of delicacies to eat.

Weary, Chester soon felt called to the
rowboat, the one with only one oar. Chester
climbed into the rowboat with Cheater at his
heels, took the oar, and shoved off the shore.
Grandfather's voice played in his mind, so
Chester positioned himself correctly in the
boat and handled the oar exactly as he had
been taught.

Chester knew that many other people
had two oars, but he could remember his
grandfather only ever having one. So having
two oars seemed one too many, on days like
these.

Cheater caught sight of Pesky following alongside the boat and gave a low, throaty growl, causing the squirrel to swim back to the oak and up, up, up its bark to safety. But as soon as the boat was in the water, Pesky resumed the chase.

Chester wondered what Cheater would do if she ever caught up with Pesky......certain they would all miss the squirrel's comical behavior if it were not there.

Chester lifted the oar and pushed it
backward through the water, causing the
boat to glide. He used the oar, skillfully, on
one side of the boat and then the other,
depending on which direction he wanted to
travel.

Cheater panted hard, anticipating what
Chester had planned. "Well done!" the old
dog thought, giving her young master a look
of approval- just the way she always had with
her old master.

Grandfather had taught Chester to fish, to swim, and to smell an oncoming storm in the air. But there was no storm in the air on this day. The waters were calm, and the sun baked Chester's flesh the way it always did, on days like these.

Chester rowed and rowed until his spirit began to lift with each rise of the oar.

Lonely, Pesky followed the boat but kept at
a safe distance. The squirrel did not want to
rile Cheater, because one never knew what
the old dog would do. Cheater was known
to suddenly chase down a nearby squirrel or
groundhog, surprising everyone and shattering
their illusion that she was sleeping and unaware
of the goings-on around her.

The great oaks were now small in the distance, and Pesky continued to follow the boat. Pesky's presence so far out on the lake assured Chester that the lake was free of unfriendly inhabitants and confirmed that it was, indeed, a wonderful day for a row on the lake.

Chester had learned that animals revealed important information about the environment, and he had been taught to listen and watch, as he did on this day.

When the boat reached the middle of
the lake, Chester placed the oar down,
carefully, and jumped into the water to
be cooled, at last, by the soothing stream.
Cheater followed close at the boy's heels,
the way she always did.

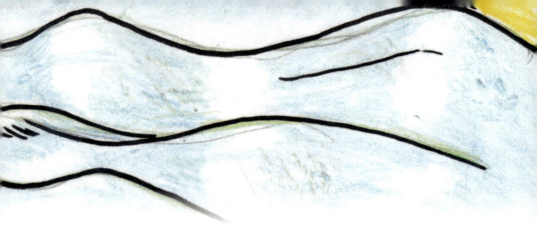

After catching sight of Pesky, Cheater swam
toward her. But Chester yelled, "Leave Pesky
be!" Just to be certain, Pesky stopped and
made ready to reverse direction, not wanting
to be cheated of life by the old dog who was
still quite full of fight.

Chester watched the fish jump in and out
of the water and challenged Cheater to a
swimming match. Tired of swimming, Chester
found a twig in the boat and threw it as far as
he could into the distance. He sent Cheater
to fetch it, which she did, obediently, each
and every time.

Chester remembered how Grandfather had played fetch with Cheater and knew that the dog missed his steady aim.

Chester remembered his feelings of bewilderment each time Cheater would follow an unspoken directive issued by his grandfather, as though man and dog could read each other's minds.

Although he had been a man of very few words, there was great purpose in every breath grandfather took, in every gesture he made, and in every word he spoke.

Chester studied the dog and knew that he was not the only one who hungered for grandfather's presence, on this day.

Having run out of games to play, Chester floated on his back and then on his stomach, until his sadness caught up with him, causing tears to well up in his eyes.

Chester remembered his grandfather's
advice the first time his parents left
him in Lockjaw for the summer: "Well,
son, sometimes you just have to cry."
Grandfather was right.

Chester let his tears flow freely, without
interruption, from his face into the lake.
He even sobbed a little as he felt the
need.

After a while, Chester felt better and somehow lighter. He was ready to return home to his parents, his grandmother, and his friends. He swam to the boat and climbed in followed by Cheater.

Once in the boat, Cheater shook, vigorously, rocking the boat from side to side to rid herself of the water that weighed her down. Pesky was nowhere in sight, having returned to the oaks to find nourishment.

Chester leaned back in the boat and placed his grandfather's hat over his face as a shield from the sun. The hat smelled like his grandfather. The aroma was neither good nor bad. It was the smell of his grandfather's life and love.

Chester now smiled, because under the hat, he could smell slices of the honey-dipped apples his grandfather used to feed him beneath the willows and oaks. Chester inhaled these smells so deeply that he fell into a calm and magical slumber. He dreamed that Cheater and Pesky were in the boat with him and that they were all the best of friends.

Chester's sleep was delicious, and he
dreamed that the planting hat was so large
that he and Grandfather wore it together, at
the same time. He dreamed that the sun, the
moon, the stars, and a rainbow were all in the
sky together, and that the fish flew as high as
the moon. He dreamed that Cheater rowed
the boat with only one oar. He dreamed
of the toothless grin that Grandfather rarely
displayed, except when Chester was with him.

Although Grandfather was sorely missed, Chester knew that everything would be all right as long as he remembered the lessons Grandfather had taught him. Chester was an expert swimmer, rower, and fisherman, and a good and honest son and friend. He had a kind heart and cared about people and animals.

Chester knew that if he remembered these lessons, he would always remember his grandfather, which brought him happiness on that day, and all the days that followed.

ABOUT THE AUTHOR

CYNTHIA STEPHENS is a native New Yorker, with maternal roots from Charleston, South Carolina. She is a playwright who has written The Princess and the Golden Yam, Nineteen Secrets and Painted Red. She believes that the most precious gift a child can receive is a book. On Days Like These is her first book.